FLANNEL FISHING SHACK COOKBOOK

By Tim Murphy

Second Edition

Copyright 2016
Shamrock Arrow Media

**For more information on
Flannel John's Cookbooks for Guys
and other titles visit
www.flanneljohn.com**

FLANNEL JOHN'S FISHING SHACK COOKBOOK

TABLE OF CONTENTS

CLAMS & CRAB

CALIFORNIA CLAM CHOWDER

6 clams, finely chopped (save clam juice)
¼ pound of bacon
1 quart of milk
2½ cups of potatoes, diced
2 cups of boiling water
2 onions, diced
2 tablespoons of butter
½ cup of celery, diced
¼ teaspoon of white pepper
½ teaspoon of salt
Cornstarch (optional)

In a skillet, fry bacon until crisp and add onions. Sauté for 5 minutes. Add celery, potatoes and seasonings. Add water, cover, and simmer for 20 minutes. Add clams, clam juice, followed by milk and butter. Heat and stir. Thicken with cornstarch if you like. Keep stirring until creamy and hot.

CLAMS & PASTA

8 ounces of clams
1 pound of fettuccine noodles
2 onions, diced
3 tablespoons of margarine
4 cloves of garlic, minced
4 tomatoes, coarsely chopped
¼ cup of wine
1 teaspoon of parsley, chopped

Cook noodles according to package directions until tender. Sauté onions in margarine until tender. Add parsley, wine, garlic, tomatoes and clams. Simmer for 20 minutes, stirring occasionally. Combine fettuccine noodles, toss and mix.

CLAM BURGERS

1 pint of razor clam necks, uncooked
2 eggs
1 teaspoon of parsley flakes
2½ teaspoons of onion flakes
4 drops of Tabasco or hot sauce of choice
2 teaspoons of Worcestershire sauce
¼ teaspoon of pepper
1 teaspoon of biscuit mix
3 saltine crackers
Butter
Hamburger buns

Grind the clams. Beat the eggs and add parsley flakes, dried onion flakes, Tabasco, Worcestershire sauce, pepper and biscuit mix. Crumble saltine crackers and add all of these ingredients to ground, mixed clams and mix well. Form small patties and fry in ½ to 1 inch of oil in a pan. Brown the patties on both sides. Serve on hamburger buns.

CLAM CAKES

1 pint of razor clam necks, uncooked
2 eggs
1 teaspoon of parsley flakes
2½ teaspoon of onion flakes
2 drops of Tabasco sauce
2 teaspoons of Worcestershire sauce
¼ teaspoon of pepper
1 teaspoon of biscuit mix
3 saltine crackers

Grind clams. Beat the eggs and combine with parsley flakes, onion, Tabasco, Worcestershire sauce, pepper and biscuit mix. Crush saltine crackers. Add everything except oil, to the ground clams and mix well. Form into small patties and fry in ½-inch of oil in a skillet. Brown well on one side and turn to brown the other side.

CLAM CASSEROLE

18 ounces of clamed, minced and drained
18 saltine crackers, coarsely crushed
4 eggs, well beaten
½ cup of milk
½ cup of onion, diced
¼ cup of green pepper, diced
¼ cup of butter, melted
1 teaspoon of salt

Mix all ingredients thoroughly and pour into a well-buttered slow cooker. Cook on low for 4 to 5 hours.

CLAM DIP

12 ounces of canned clams,
   chopped & drained
1 pint of cottage cheese, small curd
1 pint of sour cream
1½ ounces of poppy seeds
1½ ounces of toasted onion
1 tablespoon of sesame seeds
¼ teaspoon of celery seeds
Garlic powder to taste
Seasoning salt to taste

Mix together cottage cheese, onion and seeds. Add garlic powder and seasoning salt to taste. Stir in clams and mix thoroughly. Cover and refrigerate for 3 hours.

CLAM FRITTERS

1 cup of clams, diced
1 cup of flour
1 egg, beaten
½ cup of clam juice or milk
1 teaspoon of baking powder
1 teaspoon of salt

Sift flour, baking powder and salt. Beat eggs with liquid and gradually stir in to dry ingredients. Add clams into the mixture and coat thoroughly. Drop spoonfuls of clams into hot oil in a deep skillet or deep fryer. Cook until golden brown.

CLAM SOUFFLE

1 cup of minced clams
12 crackers
1 cup of milk
¼ cup of melted butter
2 beaten eggs
Salt and pepper to taste

Pour milk over cracker crumbs and let it soak. Add crackers and remaining ingredients together in a greased baking dish. Bake at 350 degrees for 30 to 40 minutes.

CLAM SOUP

1 tablespoon of olive oil
1 onion, sliced
2 potatoes, diced
1 teaspoon of salt
¼ teaspoon of black pepper
¼ teaspoon of basil
1 cup of water
6 ounces of minced clams with liquid
2 cups of milk

Heat oil in a saucepan over medium heat. Add onions, cook and stir until translucent. Stir in potatoes, salt, pepper, basil and water. Cover and bring to a boil. Reduce to a simmer. Cook for 15 minutes. Add in milk and clams with their liquid. Bring almost to a simmer while stirring frequently.

CRAB & BROCCOLI

½ cup of cooked crabmeat
1 onion, diced
¾ cup of broccoli
1 can of cream of vegetable soup
½ cup of milk
½ cup of water
2 tablespoons of butter
1/8 teaspoon of thyme

Sauté onion in butter and thyme until tender. Blend in soup, milk and water. Add flakes crab and broccoli. Cook on low heat until thoroughly warmed.

CRAB & EGGPLANT

1 pound of crabmeat
1 large eggplant, peeled and diced
16 ounces of tomato sauce
3 eggs, beaten
½ cup of breadcrumbs
3 tablespoons of butter
Juice from 1 lemon
Salt and pepper

Put eggplant in a skillet, sprinkle with lemon juice and cover with water. Cook over medium heat for about 10 minutes or until barely tender. Drain and put eggplant in a baking dish. Layer crabmeat on top of the eggplant. Pour beaten eggs and tomato sauce on top of crab. Sprinkle with breadcrumbs and dot with butter. Bake at 350 degrees for 20 to 25 minutes.

CRAB & SHRIMP SALAD

1 loaf of white bread (with ends cut off)
1 grated onion
1 cup of celery, chopped
4 hard-boiled eggs, chopped
1 cup of shrimp, small
½ cup of crab meat, chopped or shredded
2 cups of mayonnaise or Miracle Whip
Juice from 1 lemon

Butter the bread and cut into cubes. Put into a large bowl and mix well with remaining ingredients, sprinkling the lemon juice last. Refrigerate overnight or for at least 8 hours.

CRAB BAKE

1 pound of crabmeat
1 onion, diced
1 green pepper, diced
1 can of tomato soup
1 cup of mayonnaise
3 tablespoons of oil
Breadcrumbs
Butter

In a skillet, brown onion and green pepper in oil. Pour in tomato soup and mayonnaise. Stir well, add crabmeat and mix thoroughly. Pour into baking dish, sprinkle with breadcrumbs and dot or drizzle with butter. Bake at 350 degrees for 15 to 20 minutes.

CRAB CAKES

1 pound of crab cakes
½ cup of soft breadcrumbs
1 egg, beaten
2 tablespoons of mayonnaise
2 tablespoons of cream
1 tablespoon of parsley
2 tablespoons of butter, melted
1 teaspoon of Worcestershire
1 teaspoon of mustard
Salt and pepper
Flour
2 tablespoons of butter
Oil

Combine first 11 ingredients, salt and pepper to taste. Form into patties and dredge lightly in flour. Fry patties in a skillet in oil and butter mixture. When medium brown, turn cake and brown other side.

CRAB DIP

6 ounces of cream cheese
¼ cup of fresh crabmeat
1 tablespoon of onion, minced
2 tablespoons of milk
¼ teaspoon of horseradish
Garlic powder to taste

Combine all ingredients thoroughly and bake at 400 degrees for 20 minutes.

CRAB OMELET

½ cup of crab, shredded or flaked
½ cup of mushroom soup
4 eggs, beaten
1 tablespoon of milk
Salt and pepper
Butter

Melt butter in a frying pan. Pour in beaten eggs and cook slowly with a lid on the pan. Heat crab and mushroom soup together in a separate pan. Flip egg mixture and place crab mixture on top and fold over. Cover and cook 2 minutes.

CRAB SANDWICH

½ pound of fresh crabmeat
1 cup of tomato soup
½ onion, grated
2 teaspoons of mayonnaise
½ pound of Cheddar cheese, grated
6 English muffins or bagels

Mix first five ingredients and spreads on muffin or bagel halves. Bake at 350 degrees for 12 minutes.

FLORIDA KEYS DIP

8 ounces of cream cheese
1 cup of fresh crabmeat (or lobster)
1 cup of sour cream
2 crushed cloves of garlic
1 chopped green onion
4 tablespoons of mayonnaise
1 teaspoon of lime juice
Salt and pepper to taste

Put ingredients in a blender. Serve dip with crackers or fresh vegetables.

KITCHEN SINK CRAB BAKE

2 cups of crabmeat, flaked or shredded
4 ounces of canned mushrooms with liquid
1 can of mushroom soup
½ cup of mayonnaise
½ cup of milk
1 cup of cleaned shrimp
1 cup of albacore
1 cup of soft bread crumbs
2 cups of cooked rice
2 tablespoons of green pepper, diced
2 tablespoons of green onion, diced
2 eggs beaten
2 tablespoons of capers (optional)

Gently combine all ingredients in a greased baking dish. Bake at 350 degrees for 35 to 45 minutes.

OREGON CLAM FRITTERS

18 ounces of canned clams, minced & drained
2 eggs, beaten
¼ cup of onion, diced
2 cups of cornflakes, coarsely crushed
3 tablespoons of butter
¼ teaspoon of garlic powder
1/8 teaspoon of dill weed

Mix all ingredients thoroughly, except butter, and form into ½-inch patties. Heat butter in a skillet over medium heat. Fry patties slowly until golden brown on both sides.

OVEN SMOKED CLAMS

10 razor clams, diced large
½ cup of oil
1 tablespoon of liquid smoke
2 tablespoons of Worcestershire sauce
2 tablespoons of lemon juice, fresh squeezed
1 tablespoon of seasoning salt
1 tablespoon of chili powder
1 tablespoon of celery salt
1 tablespoon of garlic powder

In a bowl combine the oil and seasonings thoroughly. Stir in the clam pieces. Spread everything on a rimmed cookie sheet or shallow pan. Bake at 350 degrees for 1 hour. Stir and drain frequently, saving the liquid.

RAZOR CLAM CHOWDER

1 pint of razor clams with liquid
1 quart of milk
4 potatoes, diced
1 onion, finely diced
4 sliced of bacon, diced
Salt and pepper to taste

Fry bacon until golden brown and drain the grease. Add the bacon to the clams. In a pot, brown onion slightly then add clams, bacon and potatoes. Cover with water and simmer until potatoes are cooked. Pour in milk and season to taste. Heat until piping hot but not boiling.

FISH

ALMOND-CRUSTED ALBACORE

1½ pounds albacore steaks, skinless and
    1-inch thick
1 cup of buttermilk
½ cup of almonds, toasted and ground
½ cup of toasted bread crumbs
1 teaspoon of grated orange peel
Whole berry cranberry sauce

Wash fish in cold water and pat dry. Soak fish in buttermilk for 20 minutes. Mix toasted almonds, breadcrumbs and orange peel together. Remove fish from buttermilk and dredge in toasted almond mixture. Place on a greased baking sheet and bake at 425 degrees for 6 to 8 minutes. Albacore should be pink in the center when removed from heat. Serve with cranberry sauce.

ALMOST LIKE DEEP-FRIED FISH

1 pound of fish fillets
2 tablespoons of oil
½ cup of cornflake crumbs
Pepper, fresh ground

Wash and pat dry fillets. Make sure bones are removed. Cut into bite-size pieces. Season with pepper, dip in oil and roll in crumbs. Arrange pieces in a lightly oiled baking dish and bake at 500 degrees for 10 minutes. Do not turn or baste.

ANGLER'S BAKED SALMON

4 pound salmon fillet
½ pound of butter
1 garlic clove, crushed
¼ cup of ketchup
4 teaspoons of soy sauce
2 teaspoons of mustard
1 tablespoon of lemon juice
Worcestershire sauce
Pepper

Place salmon fillet skin-side down on a foil-lined cookie sheet. Mix remaining ingredients in a saucepan and heat to a simmer. Do not let boil. Pour mixture over the fish and bake at 350 degrees for 35 to 40 minutes.

BAKED HALIBUT

2 pounds of halibut steaks, 1-inch thick
½ cup of green onions with tops
1 cup of sour cream
¼ teaspoon of pepper
½ teaspoon of salt
¼ cup of Parmesan or Cheddar cheese

Place halibut in a buttered baking dish. Combine onion, sour cream, pepper and salt and pour mixture over the fish. Bake at 350 degrees for 20 minutes. Sprinkle with cheese and put fish in broiler just long enough to brown cheese lightly.

BAKED SALMON

3 pound salmon fillet with skin
1 lemon, sliced ¼-inch thick
1 onion, thinly sliced
Non-stick cooking oil spray

Spray baking dish with non-stick oil. Place 3 lemon slices and 3 onion slices in the dish. Put fish on top of lemon and onion. Place 2 pieces of lemon and 2 pieces of onion inside the fish. Place remainder of lemon and onion on top of fish. Cover with foil. Bake at 350 degrees for 90 minutes. Remove lemon and onion, carefully remove skin and lift fish from bones.

BAKED TILAPIA

1½ pounds of Tilapia fillets
8 ounces of sour cream
¼ cup of Parmesan cheese
2 tablespoons of butter
½ teaspoon of salt
½ teaspoon of paprika
¼ teaspoon of pepper
2 tablespoons of Italian seasoned
   breadcrumbs

Place fillets on a lightly greased pan or baking dish. Mix sour cream, cheese, paprika, salt and pepper together and spread evenly over the fish. Sprinkle with breadcrumbs and drizzle with butter. Bake at 350 degrees for 20 to 25 minutes.

BAKED WALLEYE

½ pound of walleye fillets
4 ounces of mushroom pieces, canned
2 tablespoons of sour cream
2 tablespoons of mayonnaise
¼ stick of butter
Salt and pepper to taste

Place the fish in a greased baking dish. Combine remaining ingredients thoroughly and spread over the fish. Bake at 350 degrees for 20 to 25 minutes.

BEER BATTERED PERCH

1 pound of perch, cut into 1-inch pieces
1 cup of flour
1 cup of warm beer (not dark)
1 tablespoon of dry yeast
½ teaspoon of salt
24 ounces of oil (if using a deep fryer)

Mix yeast, flour and salt with ½ cup of the beer and stir until smooth. Add the remainder of the beer and continue to stir until smooth. Let batter stand fort 30 minutes and stir batter again. Dip perch into batter and deep fry in oil at 350 degrees. If using a skillet, fry in oil on medium to high heat until golden brown.

BLACK COD TERIYAKI

5 black cod medium fillets
3 tablespoons of teriyaki
2 tablespoons of water
1 tablespoon of sugar
1 tablespoon of oil
¼ teaspoon of MSG
Green onions
Flour
Salt and pepper

Rinse and pat dry fillets. Combine flour, salt and pepper and lightly dredge each fillet. Fry fish with oil in a skillet until lightly browned. Pour off oil from pan. Combine teriyaki, water, sugar and MSG and pour over fish with sliced green onions. On low heat, simmer for 5 minutes or until fish is done.

BROILED ALBACORE

1½ pounds of skinless albacore,
    cut into 1-inch steaks
1 tablespoon of oil
2 tablespoons of lime juice
1 teaspoon of Worcestershire sauce
1½ teaspoons of dry mustard
2 teaspoons of grated lime peel

Rinse fish in cold water and pat dry. Combine oil, lime juice, mustard and Worcestershire sauce to use for basting. Place albacore on a greased broiler pan and baste with sauce. Broil 5 inches from heat for 6 to 8 minutes. Baste frequently. Turn fish halfway through cooking and continue to baste. Albacore should be pink in the center when removed from heat. Top with grated lime peel.

BROILED MAHI MAHI

2 pounds of Mahi Mahi, 6 fillets
½ cup of frozen orange juice concentrate
¼ cup of oil
¼ cup of apple cider vinegar
¼ cup of teriyaki sauce
1 tablespoon of lemon juice
½ teaspoon of salt

Combine all ingredients and marinate fish in the liquid for 2 hours in the refrigerator. Broil 4 inches from heat for 5 minutes. Turn fish, brush with sauce and broil for 5 more minutes or until lightly browned.

CAJUN CATFISH

2 pounds of catfish fillets (4 to 8 pieces)
3 tablespoons of dried parsley
1 teaspoon of garlic powder
1 teaspoon of onion salt
1 teaspoon of lemon pepper
½ teaspoon of celery salt
½ teaspoon of paprika
8 ounces of tomato sauce
2 tablespoons of oil
1 tablespoon of vinegar
1 tablespoon of Parmesan cheese, grated
Salt and pepper to taste

Combine all ingredients thoroughly except fish and cheese. Place catfish fillets in a baking dish and brush with sauce mixture then sprinkle with Parmesan cheese. Bake at 350 degrees for 40 minutes or until fish flakes easily.

CARIBBEAN ALBACORE

1½ pounds of skinless 1-inch albacore steaks
½ cup of plain, low fat yogurt
½ teaspoon of curry powder
2 tablespoons of vegetable oil
2 tablespoons of lime juice
1 tablespoon of orange marmalade
2 teaspoons of lime juice
Salt
Fresh fruit of choice

Rinse fish in cold water and pat dry. Blend yogurt, marmalade, curry powder and 2 teaspoons of lime juice together. Chill for 30 minutes. Combine oil, 2 tablespoons of lime juice and a pinch or two of salt. Baste albacore with the oil mixture. Place fish on well-greased grate 5 to 6 inches from hot coals. Cook 8 minutes per inch of thickness, measured at thickest point. Turn fish once and baste frequently. Albacore should be pink in the center when removed from heat. Serve with yogurt sauce. Garnish with fresh fruit of choice…strawberries, melon, grapes, oranges, etc.

CHEESY FLOUNDER

1½ pounds of flounder, 4 fillets
4 ounces of sharp Cheddar cheese
4 scallions, chopped
16 ounces of tomato sauce
½ teaspoon of oregano
¼ teaspoon of salt
Pepper to taste

Cut fish into 4 pieces. Put a slice of cheese on each piece of fish. Sprinkle scallions, oregano, salt and pepper over fish. Roll up each fillet and secure with a toothpick. Place fillets in a greased baking dish and cover with tomato sauce. Bake at 350 degrees for 20 minutes.

COD WITH TOMATO

1 ½ pounds of cod fillets
1 ½ cups of water
2 tablespoons of lemon juice
2 large tomatoes, sliced ¼-inch thick
¼ teaspoon of pepper
½ green pepper, finely diced
2 tablespoons of onion, finely diced
¼ cup of dry breadcrumbs
½ teaspoon of basil
1 tablespoon of oil

Put fish in a bowl and pour a mixture of water and lemon juice over the fillets. Let stand for 30 minutes. Place fish in a lightly oil baking dish. Season with pepper. Top with tomato slices and sprinkle with green pepper and onion. Combine breadcrumbs, basil and oil thoroughly. Spread the mixture over the tomatoes. Bake at 350 degrees for 25 minutes or until fish is firm and flakes with a fork.

CURSES, FOILED AGAIN FISH

4 fish fillets, ¼ pound to ½ pound each,
   cleaned and de-boned
1 onion, diced
1 stalk of celery (celery salt can be used)
1 green pepper, diced
4 pats of butter
Salt and pepper

Place each fillet on a piece of aluminum foil big enough to fully wrap each fish. Add in onion, green pepper and celery (or celery salt). Salt and pepper to taste. Top with a pat of butter. Wrap tightly and bake directly on hot coals or grill for 15 to 20 minutes. This makes for a great campfire dinner.

FINNISH SALMON STEW

8 ounces of canned red salmon,
   cleaned, de-boned and in chunks
1 onion, diced
4 allspice, whole
1/3 stick of butter, sliced
1 bay leaf
Salt to taste
Water to cover

Put potatoes, onions, allspice and bay leaf in a large pot. Pour in just enough water to cover. Heat on high for 15 to 20 minutes until potatoes are nearly done. Add salmon and butter to the pot plus salt to taste. Reduce heat to a simmer. Cover and cook for 5 to 10 minutes until potatoes are tender and salmon is hot.

FISH & CATTAILS

2 quarts of cattail shoots or young stems,
  washed
4 bass or trout fillets
2 cups of water
Salt to taste
Crushed red pepper, to taste

Harvest spring cattail shoots or green, new stems. Put fish fillets in a skillet and lay cattails on tops. Pour water into the skillet and cover. Steam for 5 to 10 minutes. Season to taste with salt and crushed red pepper.

FISH & CHIPS

2 pounds of white fish
  (I prefer fresh albacore or halibut)
1 cup of flour
2 teaspoons of baking powder
1 teaspoon of salt
½ cup of warm water
1 egg, separated
1 tablespoon of melted fat
Oil for deep fryer

In a deep fryer, heat oil or shortening to 400 degrees. Oil should be 4 to 6 inches deep. Cut fish into serving pieces. Sift flour, baking powder and salt into a bowl. Drop egg yolk in the center. Add water and fat then mix well. Blend in the beaten egg white and mix thoroughly. Dry the fish pieces and dip in batter. Slide pieces into the hot oil and fry until golden brown.

FISH CHOWDER

1 pound of haddock or cod fillets,
  cut into small pieces
1½ cups of water
½ cup of milk
1 tablespoon of butter
¾ cup of onion, diced
1 clove of garlic
1 bay leaf
1 sprig of parsley
½ teaspoon of thyme
Fresh ground black pepper

Melt butter in a pan and sauté onions and garlic. Add in remaining ingredients and simmer for 45 minutes.

FISH HEAD STEW

1 salmon head
1 skein of salmon row
½ piece of salmon backbone
5 chunks of salmon
1 salmon tail
4 potatoes, peeled and diced
2 cups of celery, diced
1 onion, diced
1 can of corn
Salt and pepper to taste
Water

Put salmon head, salmon row, celery, onion, potato, salmon chunks, salmon backbone, corn and salmon tail in a stew pot. Add in enough water to cover 2 inches above the ingredients. Boil until potatoes and fish are done. Salt and pepper to taste. Watch out for small bones.

FISHING PARTY SALMON BAKE

6 pound salmon fillet
Juice from 2 lemons
¼ cup of melted butter
2 tablespoons of dry sherry
Salt
White pepper
Garlic salt
Oregano
Chopped parsley

Place the salmon skin side down on a cooking tray and squeeze the juice from both lemons over the fish. Sprinkle with salt, pepper and garlic salt to taste. Pour melted butter over seasoned fish and top with chopped parsley. Sprinkle sherry over everything. Bake at 350 degrees for 30 minutes. Fish should be opaque and flake easily when cooked.

FRIED PERCH

1 pound of perch fillets
2 tablespoons of egg substitute
½ cup of white cornmeal
4 tablespoons of olive oil

Clean and de-bone fillets. At fish with egg substitute and press into cornmeal, thoroughly coating both sides and edges. Heat 2 tablespoons of oil in a skillet over medium heat. Add fillets and additional oil if needed. Fry until lightly browned and crisp then turn and repeat. When finished place fish on paper towels and blot to remove excess oil.

GRILLED CITRUS SALMON

1½ pound salmon fillet
¼ cup of packed brown sugar
½ teaspoon of dill
½ teaspoon of lemon pepper
¼ teaspoon of garlic powder
3 tablespoons of chicken broth
3 tablespoons of oil
3 tablespoons of soy sauce
3 tablespoons of green onion, finely chopped
1 lemon thinly sliced
2 onion slices

Sprinkle dill, lemon pepper and garlic [powder over salmon fillet. Place in a baking dish. Combine broth, oil, soy sauce, brown sugar and green onions; then pour over fish. Cover and refrigerate for 2 hours, turning once. Place salmon skin side down on a grill with medium heat. Place lemon and separated onion rings on top of fish. Cover and cook for 1 to 20 minutes or until fish flakes easily with a fork. You can also bake the fish in an over at 350 degrees for 16 to 24 minutes.

GRILLED SNAPPER

1 pound of snapper (2 fillets, cleaned)
3 tablespoons of soy sauce
2 tablespoons of lemon juice
½ teaspoon of dried tarragon, ground
½ teaspoon of dried cilantro, ground
½ teaspoon of paprika, ground
½ teaspoon of garlic powder
1 tablespoon of sesame oil
Can of non-stick cooking spray

Put fillets in a baking dish and sprinkle with lemon juice and soy sauce. Turn fish to coat evenly. Put dish in refrigerator for 1 hour, turning once. Spray grill or fry pan with non-stick cooking oil, then sprinkle with sesame oil. Bring grill or pan to medium heat. Sprinkle ½ the spice mixture on the fish and place spice side down on the heat. After 5 to 6 minutes, sprinkle remaining spices on fish and flip. Cook for another 5 to 6 minutes or until fillets begin to flake.

HALIBUT CREOLE

3 halibut steaks
4 ounces of mushrooms
3 tablespoons of butter
½ cup of onion, diced
1 cup of ketchup
1 clove of garlic
¼ cup of green pepper, diced
¼ cup of water
½ cup of wine
1 tablespoon of lemon juice
½ teaspoon of salt

In a skillet heat butter and brown onion, garlic and green pepper. Mix with remaining ingredients in a bowl to make a sauce. Put fish in a greased baking dish. Pour sauce over fish. Bake at 375 degrees for 40 minutes.

HALIBUT STEAK

1½ pounds of halibut, ½-inch thick
1 small onion
½ stick of butter (more or less if you prefer)
Juice from ½ lemon
¼ cup of sour cream
½ cup of grated cheddar cheese
Salt and pepper

Place fish in baking dish. Sprinkle salt and pepper over steaks. Cut onion into rings and place on fish. In a pan, melt butter and add sour cream and lemon. Blend and pour the mixture over the halibut. Sprinkle cheese on top and bake at 350 degrees for 35 minutes.

ITALIAN FISH FILLETS

2 pounds of fish fillets, fresh or thawed
8 ounces of spaghetti sauce with mushrooms
2 tablespoons of chopped onion
1 cup of shredded mozzarella cheese
Salt

Place fillets on a greased baking sheet. Salt to taste. Mix spaghetti sauce with onion and pour over fish. Bake uncovered at 350 degrees for 25 to 30 minutes, or until fish flakes easily. Sprinkle with cheese and bake for another 3 minutes or until cheese is melted.

MOCK LOBSTER

2 pounds of halibut, cut into 2-inch squares
4 cups of water
3½ tablespoons of salt
6 tablespoons of sugar
Melted butter

Add sugar and salt to water and bring to a boil. Reduce heat, add in halibut and simmer for 5 minutes. Serve with melted butter.

NORTHERN PIKE

4 8-ounce Northern Pike fillets
1 cup of milk
1 green onion, diced fine
1 tablespoon of fresh parsley, diced fine
½ cup of butter, melted
½ cup of dry breadcrumbs
½ teaspoon of salt
½ teaspoon of pepper

Put fillets in a bowl with milk and soak for 30 minutes in the refrigerator. Mix breadcrumbs, salt, pepper and parsley thoroughly. Remove fish from milk and dredge in breadcrumb mixture until completely coated. Place fish in a lightly greased baking dish. Sprinkle green onion over fish and drizzle with melted butter. Bake at 350 degrees for 25 minutes or until fish flakes easily.

ORANGE ROUGHY WITH BASIL

2 pounds of orange roughy, 8 fillets
½ cup of chicken broth
½ cup of dry sherry
3 tomatoes, peeled and sliced
2 tablespoons of butter
2 tablespoons of flour
2 tablespoons of fresh chives, chopped
½ teaspoon of dried basil
½ teaspoon of dried thyme
½ teaspoon of salt
¼ teaspoon of pepper

Melt butter in a saucepan over low heat and stir in flour until smooth. Cook for 1 minute while stirring. Gradually add in broth and sherry and cook over medium heat. Continue to stir until mixture thickens and is bubbly. Stir in chives, basil and thyme then set aside. Place fillets in a lightly greased baking dish and sprinkle with salt and pepper. Place tomato slices on fillets and spoon sauce over tomatoes and fillets. Bake at 300 degrees for 30 to 40 minutes, until fish flakes with a fork.

PEPPERED TROUT

2 pounds of trout
2 cups of cooked tomatoes
2 cups of potato balls
1 cup of mushrooms
1 clove of garlic
1 red pepper pod
1 onion, minced
½ cup of olive oil
1 tablespoon of Worcestershire sauce
1 tablespoon of vinegar
Salt and pepper to taste

Sprinkle trout with salt and pepper. Put garlic and pepper pod inside the fish. Place onion and fish in a pan or baking dish and cover with tomatoes. Add Worcestershire sauce, vinegar, olive oil and potato balls. Bake at 400 degrees for 15 minutes. Add mushrooms and bake for an additional 15 minutes or until fish and potatoes are tender.

POACHED FLOUNDER

1 pound of flounder fillets
1 onion, sliced into rings
1 tablespoon of lemon juice
1 clove of garlic, chopped
½ teaspoon of salt
¼ teaspoon of pepper
¼ cup of water

Put flounder in a baking dish and cover with onion rings and garlic. Mix water, lemon juice, salt and pepper and pour over fish. Cover the fish with foil and bake at 350 degrees for 15 minutes or until fish easily flakes.

POACHED SALMON STEAKS

1 pound of salmon steaks
¾ cup of water
¾ cup of dry white wine
1 onion, chopped
¼ teaspoon of pepper
1/8 teaspoon of cloves
1/8 teaspoon of thyme
1 bay leaf

Place salmon in a skillet. Mix remaining ingredients thoroughly and add to the pan. If needed, add additional water so fish is barely covered with liquid. Simmer over low heat for 15 to 20 minutes or until salmon is firm and flakes with a fork. Drain liquid, remove bay leaf and serve.

QUICK BARBECUED FISH

8 fish fillets, cleaned and de-boned
2 cups of French dressing
3 cups of cracker crumbs

Dip fillets in dressing and coat with cracker crumbs. Put fillets on a grill about 5 inches from the coals. Brush with more dressing. Cook 3 to 4 minutes per side but be careful not to over cook. You can also bake in the oven at 350 degrees for 12 to 20 minutes.

RAINBOW TROUT AMANDINE

6 rainbow trout, filleted and slit on the side
2 sticks of butter
3 lemons
1 package of toasted almonds
Parsley

Inside fish, fill with pats of butter from ½ stick, thin slices from 1 lemon and chopped parsley. Place each fish in an aluminum foil basket and cover with pats of butter from ½ stick, parsley and thin slices from one lemon. Close up the foil baskets and bake each fish at 400 degrees. After 25 minutes, uncover fish and cook fort an additional 15 minutes or until trout is brown and crispy on the outside. In a pan, melt the remaining stick of butter, add juice from the last lemon and mix in almonds. Heat slowly for a few minutes. When ready to serve, pour sauce over fish.

ROCKFISH WITH MUSHROOMS

1 pound of rockfish fillets
½ teaspoon of salt
½ teaspoon of MSG (optional)
¼ cup of flour or cracker crumbs
2 tablespoons of butter
½ cup of canned mushrooms, drained
1 cup of sour cream (at room temperature)
1 tablespoon of flour

Dry fillets with paper towel and season with salt and MSG. Coat with flour or cracker crumbs. In a large skillet, heat butter until melted then add the fillets. Brown both sides. Allow fish to cool slightly. Mix one tablespoon of flour with sour cream and pour over the fish. Simmer very slowly uncovered for 5 to 10 minutes. Do not allow mixture to boil or sour cream will curdle.

ROYAL TUNA

1 can of tuna
1 cup of mashed potatoes
2 eggs
Salt and pepper
Oil

Combine tuna, beaten eggs and potatoes. Season with salt and pepper and mix thoroughly. Pour 1 inch of oil into a skillet and heat. Drop spoonfuls of mixture into the hot oil and fry until golden brown.

SALMON CHOWDER

2 cups of diced celery
1 onion, diced
3 carrots, grated
2 potatoes, diced
½ teaspoon of basil
1 teaspoon of salt
13 ounces of evaporated milk
2 cups of cleaned salmon pieces
Milk
Water

Combine celery, onion, carrots and potatoes in a large pan. Pour in just enough water to barely cover ingredients and add salt and basil. Cover and simmer over low to medium heat until vegetables are tender. Stir in evaporated milk. Add salmon and just enough milk to bring soup to desired consistency. Heat until small bubbles form on the inside edge of the pan.

SALMON IN FOIL

1 salmon fillet
Brown sugar
Green onions, chopped white & green parts
Melted butter
Soy Sauce

Place fillet skin side down on a large piece of aluminum foil. Spread layer of brown sugar over the fish then sprinkle green onions over the sugar. Drizzle melted butter and soy sauce over everything and close up the foil. Bake in oven or on the barbecue fort about 20 minutes until it flakes with a fork.

SALMON LOAF

1 pound of salmon, flaked
1 cup of cracker crumbs
1 cup of sweet cream
3 eggs, beaten
Salt and pepper to taste

Combine all ingredients and mix until all the cracker crumbs are moist. Bake in a loaf pan at 350 degrees for 45 minutes.

SALMON LOAF II

1 pound of salmon, canned
2 eggs, separated
1/3 cup of hot milk
1 cup of soft breadcrumbs
1 tablespoon of parsley
1 teaspoon of onion, minced
1 teaspoon of lemon juice
½ teaspoon of salt
½ teaspoon of nutmeg

Remove skin and bones from fish, flake and save the juice. Combine hot milk and breadcrumbs. Add seasonings, reserved salmon juice and egg yolks. If need, add more salt. Fold in stiffly beaten egg whites and pour everything into a greased baking dish. Bake at 350 degrees for 45 minutes or until firm in the middle and lightly browned.

SALMON PUFF

4 eggs, lightly beaten
½ cup of milk
1 can of cream of mushroom soup
1 can of salmon, medium size
2 cups of soft breadcrumbs
1 tablespoon of minced parsley
2 tablespoons of butter

Combine eggs, milk and soup. Blend in remaining ingredients and place in a buttered baking dish. Bake at 350 degrees for 45 to 50 minutes.

SALMON SOUP

4 cups of milk, scalded
2 cups of shredded salmon
2 tablespoons of butter
Salt and pepper

Combine salmon, butter and milk in a saucepan. Season to taste. Heat thoroughly and stir until well blended

SEA STEAKS WITH ROSEMARY

4 fish steaks, 1-inch thick
  (salmon, swordfish or mackerel)
½ cup of melted butter
½ teaspoon of dried rosemary
Salt and pepper

Place fish in a lightly oiled baking dish. Pour butter over fish then salt and pepper to taste. Sprinkle rosemary over the fish. Broil 4 to 6 inches from heat. Turn once until fish flakes easily, about 10 to 15 minutes.

SEAT-OF-YOUR-PANTS
STEELHEAD

1 steelhead fillet
Onion salt
MSG
Mayonnaise
Italian seasoning
Lemon pepper
Cracker crumbs
¼ stick of butter

Sprinkle fish with onion salt and MSG to taste. Spread mayo on the fish and sprinkle with Italian seasoning then dip in cracker crumbs. Melt butter and drizzle over fish. Sprinkle with lemon pepper. Bake at 425 degrees for 25 to 35 minutes.

SESAME HALIBUT

2 pounds of halibut fillets
2 tablespoons of ketchup
1 tablespoon of soy sauce
1 tablespoon of fresh-squeezed lemon juice
¼ teaspoon of pepper
¾ teaspoon of sesame oil
1 tablespoon of brown sugar
1 tablespoon of sesame seeds, toasted
¼ cup of frozen orange juice concentrate,
   thawed

Clean and rinse fish with cold water and pat dry. Cut fish into large chunks in place in a large bowl. In a small bowl, combine orange juice, ketchup, soy sauce, lemon juice, pepper, sesame oil and brown sugar. Pour mixture over fish and gently stir to coat fish chunks. Cover and place in the refrigerator to marinate for 2 to 3 hours. When ready to cook, put fish chunks on skewers. Cook over medium-hot coal or broil in an oven for 15 minutes. Turn once while cooking and baste once or twice with the marinade. When fish is cooked, it should flake with the touch of a fork. Top with toasted sesame seeds.

SKILLET FRIED TROUT

4 trout fillets
1 egg, beaten
½ cup milk
4 tablespoons of breadcrumbs or corn meal
1 teaspoon of salt
2 tablespoons of bacon fat
   (butter or olive oil can be used)
Salt and pepper
Lemon (optional)
Dill (optional)

Mix salt in milk and dip fish in the liquid. Then dip fillets in beaten eggs and roll in breadcrumbs or corn meal. Heat oil in a skillet until hot but not smoking. Fry until golden brown, turning it once.
Salt and pepper to taste. You can also use lemon or dill for seasoning.

SMELT BAKE

18 smelt, cleaned
1 cup of dry breadcrumbs
½ stick of butter
¼ teaspoon of onion powder (or less)
1/3 cup of flour
2 eggs
2 teaspoons of water
½ teaspoon of salt
Dash of pepper
Dash of salt

Melt butter with onion powder and set aside. Combine flour with ½ teaspoon of salt and dash of pepper. Make an egg wash by beating 2 eggs with water. Coat smelt with flour mixture, dip in egg wash then coat with breadcrumbs. Grease a baking dish and arrange smelt in a single layer. Drizzle butter mixture over fish and sprinkle with dash of salt to taste. Bake uncovered at 375 degrees for 15 to 20 minutes until brown.

SMOKED SALMON

3 pounds of salmon fillets,
   cut into 3-inch strips
4 cups of brown sugar
2 cups of canning salt
1 smoker

Combine sugar and salt in a large bowl and roll salmon fillets in the mixture. Place fish in a sealed plastic container. Let rest for 3 hours with thick fillets and 90 minutes for thinner cuts. Remove fish from container and put on racks to dry. Then smoke for 8 to 12 hours or until it reaches desired doneness.

SMOKED TROUT

8 - 10 trout, cleaned and de-boned
1 cup of Morton's Tender Quick
8 teaspoons of liquid smoke
½ cup of rock salt
1 gallon of water

Mix Tender Quick, liquid smoke and salt in a gallon of water. Soak fish in the mixture for 24 hours in a non-metallic container. Bake at 200 degrees for 4 hours on a lightly greased cookie sheet. Turn fish after 2 hours. To store, wrap in freezer paper and freeze.

SNAPPER AND TATERS

1½ pounds of red snapper
4 potatoes
5 tablespoons of olive oil
1½ tablespoons of dried parsley

Peel potatoes and slice ¼ thick. Place them in a baking dish. Add 3 tablespoons of oil and half the parsley and mix thoroughly with the potatoes. Bake at 400 degrees for 40 minutes. Clean and de-bone snapper fillets. Coat fish with 2 tablespoons of oil and the rest of the parsley. Place fish on top of the potatoes. Return to oven and bake at 400 degrees for 20 minutes. Fish should flake when touched with a fork when done.

SNAPPER WITH LIME

1 pound of red snapper, 2 fillets
2 limes
2 tablespoons of oil

Clean and de-bone fish fillets. Place in a baking dish and squeeze the juice of 2 limes over the fish. Cover with plastic wrap and marinate in the refrigerator for 4 hours, turning fillets every hour. When ready to cook, coat fish with oil. Bake in an uncovered dish at 400 degrees for 20 to 25 minutes.

SOLE WITH HERBS

1 pound of fillet of sole
1/3 cup of lemon juice
¼ teaspoon of dry mustard
½ teaspoon of tarragon
2 tablespoons of margarine

Spread margarine on the bottom of a baking dish and add fish. Combine lemon juice, tarragon and mustard then brush the mixture on the fish. Broil 3 inches from heat, 5 to 8 minutes for thin fillets and 10 to 12 minutes for thicker cuts. Brush a with lemon juice mixture a couple of times during the broiling. When fish is firm and flakes with a fork it is done.

SOUPED UP FISH

1 pound of fresh fish
1 can of cream of mushroom soup
¼ cup of apple juice
¼ teaspoon of curry powder

Place fish in a baking dish. Combine soup, apple juice and curry powder and pour over fish. Bake at 350 degrees for 15 to 20 minutes.

STURGEON SAUSAGE

3½ pounds of sturgeon
3½ teaspoons of lemon zest
1½ teaspoons of cayenne pepper
1½ teaspoons of white pepper
3½ teaspoons of salt
1½ teaspoons of sage
3½ teaspoons of parsley, chopped
1½ teaspoons of garlic, minced
4 feet of sausage casing, 1-inch diameter

Put sturgeon through the finest setting on the meat grinder. Add remaining ingredients and mix thoroughly in a stainless steel bowl with a rubber spatula. Grind mixture again. Tightly wrap the mixture and let it rest overnight in the refrigerator. Stuff the sausage into casings. Tie off 3-inch links and pierce with the tip of a skewer. Cook sausage in boiling water for 7 to 8 minutes. Once cooked, plunge into ice water. Place in a refrigerator overnight in a tightly wrapped container. When ready to serve, grill boil or steam.

SWEET AND SOUR MAHI MAHI

2½ pounds of Mahi Mahi fillets
¼ cup of water
3 tablespoons of teriyaki sauce
1 tablespoon of cornstarch
1 teaspoon of ginger root, minced
2 teaspoons of sesame seeds, toasted
½ cup of sugar
½ cup of rice vinegar
¼ teaspoon of salt
¼ teaspoon of MSG

Cut fillets into 2½-inch pieces. Put fish in a baking dish. Combine teriyaki sauce, ginger, sesame seeds, sugar, rice vinegar and cornstarch dissolved in water. Pour mixture over fish. Bake in oven at 375 degrees for 14 to 20 minutes or until cooked but not overdone.

SWEET AND SOUR PERCH

1 pound of perch, 4 fillets
2 tablespoons of cornstarch
1 teaspoon of salt
3 tablespoons of oil
¼ cup of sugar
¼ cup of apple cider vinegar
3 tablespoons of soy sauce
3 tablespoons of ketchup
Non-stick cooking spray

Put cornstarch and salt in a large Ziploc bag. Place each de-boned fillet in the bag on at a time and shake to coat. Heat oil in a skillet with medium heat. Fry fish for 2½ minutes per side. Blot oil from fish with paper towels. Mix sugar, vinegar, soy sauce and ketchup in a small bowl. Microwave for 1 minute, stir and microwave for 1 additional minute. If you prefer, heat sauce mixture in a small pan, but do not let it boil. Place fish in a baking dish sprayed with non-stick oil. Pour sauce over fish and bake at 350 degrees for 15 minutes.

TEX-MEX HALIBUT

2 pounds of halibut
1 onion, diced
1 green pepper, diced
2 jalapeno peppers, seeded and chopped
1 cup of mayonnaise
½ pound of cheddar cheese, grated
Lemon pepper
Salt

Cut halibut into serving pieces and place in a baking dish. In a bowl, thoroughly mix onion, green pepper, jalapenos, mayonnaise and cheese. Spread mixture over the fish. Bake at 350 degrees for 17 to 22 minutes or until fish flakes with a fork.

TROUT WITH AN OINK

1 pound of bacon
2 onions, thinly sliced
2 fresh trout, cleaned
½ cup of corn meal
½ cup of flour
1 tablespoon of salt
1 tablespoon of pepper

Fry bacon and remove once it is crisp. Sauté onions in the bacon grease. Remove onions and lightly salt. Mix corn meal, flour, salt and pepper thoroughly and coat fish with the mixture. Fry fish in the grease until done and very crisp. Garnish with fried onion and bacon.

TUNA MAC

1 can of tuna, flaked and drained
1 cup of small macaroni
3 ounces of cream cheese
1 can of cream of mushroom soup
¼ cup of milk
1 tablespoon of mustard
1 tablespoon of onion, diced
1 small bag of potato chips, crushed
Butter

Cook macaroni and drain, then pour in a greased baking dish. Soften cream cheese and blend with the rest of the ingredients. Pour mixture over the macaroni. Top with crushed potato chips and drizzle melted butter over the top. Bake at 375 degrees for 25 minutes.

TUNA AND NOODLES

1 can of cream of mushroom soup
1 cup of milk
7 ounce can of tuna, flaked
6 ounces of chow mein noodles

Mix soup and milk in a pan and heat then add tuna. Once piping hot, pour over crisp chow mein noodles.

TUNA CASSEROLE

1 can of tuna, drained and flake
1 can of cream of celery soup
¼ cup of milk
2 hard-boiled eggs, diced
1 cup of cooked peas
½ cup of crumbled potato chips

In a greased baking dish, blend soup and milk. Stir in tuna, eggs and peas. Top with potato chip crumbs. Bake at 350 degrees for 25 minutes

WALNUT SOLE

1 pound of sole, 4 fillets
1 cup of walnuts, finely chopped
2 egg whites, lightly beaten
2 tablespoons of oil
½ cup of flour
¼ cup of cracker crumbs
¼ cup of clarified butter
½ teaspoon of salt
¼ teaspoon of pepper

Mix flour, salt and pepper. Combine walnuts and cracker crumbs. Dredge fillets in flour mixture, dip in egg whites, then dredge in walnut mixture. Fry in a skillet in a butter and oil mixture for 3 minutes per side or until golden brown.

OYSTERS

BAKED OYSTERS

1 pint of oysters
12 slices of half-cooked bacon
6 ounces of whole mushrooms, canned
1 green pepper, cut in squares
4 tablespoons of margarine, melted
1 tablespoon of lemon juice
¼ teaspoon of salt
Pepper to taste
Garlic powder to taste

Wrap oysters in bacon. Place on skewers and alternate with mushrooms and green pepper squares. Place in a baking dish. Combine remaining ingredients and brush on oysters. Bake at 450 degrees for 10 minutes.

BARBECUED OYSTERS

1 pint of oysters
½ cup of oil
½ cup of American cheese, grated fine
½ cup of dry breadcrumbs
1 clove of garlic, diced fine
1 teaspoon of salt
Hot sauce (optional)

Drain the oysters. Mix oil, salt and garlic thoroughly. Soak the oysters in the oil mixture for 1 to 2 minutes. Remove the oysters from the liquid, drain slightly and roll in the shredded cheese. Now roll in the breadcrumbs. Place the oysters on a greased baking sheet. Bake oysters at 450 degrees for 12 minutes or until browned. Remove from oven and sprinkle with hot sauce (optional).

CREAMED OYSTERS

1 dozen oysters with liquid
1 cup of milk, heated
1 tablespoon of butter
1 tablespoon of flour
1 tablespoon of parsley, minced
1 teaspoon of Worcestershire sauce
Salt and pepper to taste

In a pan, melt butter over low heat. Stir in flour until mixture is smooth. Slowly add the heated milk. Once the sauce thickens, stir in Worcestershire sauce, parsley and salt and pepper to taste. Finally add oysters and liquid. Cook over low heat for 10 minutes or until oysters are plump.

DEVILED OYSTERS

1 pint of oysters
¼ pound of butter
1 onion, diced
½ cup of celery, chopped
1 cup of cracker crumbs
1 egg, beaten
Juice of ½ lemon
Salt to taste
Cayenne pepper to taste

Heat oysters at 350 degrees until they curl then chop. Cook celery and onion in half the butter until tender. Combine with chopped oysters, ½ cup of cracker crumbs, beaten egg, salt and cayenne pepper. Put everything in a baking dish. Cover with a mixture of the remaining butter and cracker crumbs. Bake at 350 degrees until browned.

LEMON PEPPER OYSTERS

24 oysters, as fresh as possible
1 lemon, cut into wedges
Freshly ground pepper

Leave oysters on a half shell with liquid. Sprinkle each with fresh ground pepper with lemon wedges on the side.

OYSTER & VEGETABLE STEW

1 pint of shucked oysters
6 cups of chicken broth
2 tablespoons of soy sauce
1 teaspoon of ginger, grated
2 cups of chopped cabbage
8 ounces of sliced mushrooms
½ cup of bean sprouts
6 ounces of pea pods

In a pan, heat chicken broth, soy sauce and ginger until it boils. Add oysters with their liquid followed by cabbage, mushrooms, bean sprouts and pea pods. Heat to boiling and reduce heat. Cover and simmer until cabbage is tender yet crisp, 2 to 3 minutes.

OYSTER POT

1 cup of raw oysters
1 pound of raw shrimp, peeled and cleaned
½ cup of chopped green onion
½ cup of chopped white onion
1 green pepper cut into strips
½ cup of chopped celery
1 teaspoon of minced garlic
1/3 cup of butter
1 pound of canned tomatoes
1 cup of chicken broth
½ teaspoon of salt
½ teaspoon of cayenne pepper
1 cup of raw rice

In a pan or pot, sauté onion, green pepper, celery and garlic in butter until tender but not brown. Add shrimp and oysters and cook for five minutes. If you're using ham instead of oysters, add the ham with the rice. Add tomatoes, chicken broth, salt, cayenne and rice and stir then cover. Cook everything for 25 minutes over low heat or until rice is done. If mixture becomes dry, add tomato juice.

OYSTER SAUSAGE

1½ pounds of fresh oysters, raw with liquid
¾ pound of scallops, raw and drained
2 teaspoons of salt
1½ teaspoons of lemon zest
¾ teaspoon of white pepper
¾ teaspoon of cayenne pepper
½ teaspoon of ground fennel
1 cup of dry breadcrumbs
4 feet of ¾-inch sausage casing

Combine all ingredients in a food processor and run until finely chopped but not pureed. Use the breadcrumbs to adjust consistency. Let mixture rest overnight, tightly wrapped, in the refrigerator. The next day stuff mixture in casing and tie-off in 2½ to 3-inch links. Pierce each link with the tip of a skewer. Cook links in boiling water for 7 minutes then plunge into ice water. Allow links to stand overnight, tightly wrapped and refrigerated. Reheat by grilling, boiling or steaming.

OYSTER STEW

1 pint of shucked oysters
6 cups of chicken broth
2 tablespoons of soy sauce
1 teaspoon of ginger, grated
2 cups of chopped cabbage
8 ounces of sliced mushrooms
½ cup of bean sprouts
6 ounces of pea pods

In a pan, heat chicken broth, soy sauce and ginger until it boils. Add oysters with their liquid followed by cabbage, mushrooms, bean sprouts and pea pods. Heat to boiling and reduce heat. Cover and simmer until cabbage is tender yet crisp, 2 to 3 minutes.

SCALLOPED OYSTERS

1 pint of oysters
2 cups of cracker crumbs
¼ cup of butter
½ teaspoon of salt
½ teaspoon of celery salt
¼ teaspoon of paprika
1½ cups of milk

Starting with oysters, layer each ingredient in a baking dish. Bake at 350 degrees for 30 to 40 minutes.

SHRIMP

JAMBALAYA

2 pounds of shrimp, peeled and uncooked
1 pound of sausage, chopped
10 ounces of French onion soup
10 ounces of beef bouillon
8 ounces of tomato sauce
½ cup of green onion, chopped
½ cup of bell pepper, chopped
½ cup of onion, diced
½ cup of butter, softened
2 cups of rice
Garlic powder to taste
Creole/Cajun seasoning

Combine shrimp, sausage, soup and bouillon in a large pot and mix well. Stir in tomato sauce, green pepper, green onion, onion, rice and butter. Cover pot and bake at 375 degrees for 30 minutes. Stir well. Cover and bake for another 30 minutes.

BROILED SHRIMP

24 large shrimp, unshelled
1 onion, sliced thin
1 green pepper, sliced thin
1 stick of butter
½ cup of olive oil
¼ cup of chopped garlic
1 teaspoon of salt
Black pepper

Place unshelled shrimp on a small-rimmed baking sheet. Pour melted butter and olive oil over them. Sprinkle with salt and black pepper to taste. Sprinkle garlic over the top of everything. Cover with plastic wrap and refrigerate for 3 hours. Preheat the oven broiler. Place onion and green pepper slices on top of the shrimp. Broil about 4 inches from the heat for 5 minutes. Turn shrimp and broil for another 5 minutes.

CURRY SHRIMP

1½ pounds of raw, cleaned, de-veined shrimp
10 ounce can of cream of shrimp soup
10 ounce can of cream of mushroom soup
¾ cup of sour cream
1½ teaspoons of curry powder
2 tablespoons of butter

Melt butter in a pan. Add shrimp and cook 3 to 5 minutes stirring frequently. Add in soups and stir thoroughly. Stir in cream and curry powder and heat until soup is cooked.

SHRIMP BOWL

1 pound of jumbo shrimp
1 pound of scallops
2 scallions, sliced
2 tablespoons of ginger, chopped
1 tablespoon of ketchup
1 tablespoon of sherry (optional)
1 tablespoon of soy sauce
½ teaspoon of salt
½ teaspoon of crushed red pepper flakes
3 cloves of garlic
1 teaspoon of sugar
1 tablespoon of chili sauce
  (try Sriracha for some heat)

In a medium bowl, combine chili sauce, ketchup, sherry, soy sauce, pepper flakes, garlic, sugar and salt into a sauce and set aside. In a skillet cook shrimp, scallops, scallions and ginger over high heat. Drain off liquid and add sauce. Heat thoroughly while stirring.

SHRIMP & CRAB SALAD

1 loaf of white bread (with ends cut off)
1 grated onion
1 cup of celery, chopped
4 hard-boiled eggs, chopped
1 cup of shrimp, small
½ cup of crab meat, chopped or shredded
2 cups of mayonnaise or Miracle Whip
Juice from 1 lemon

Butter the bread and cut into cubes. Put into a large bowl and mix well with remaining ingredients, sprinkling the lemon juice last. Refrigerate overnight or for at least 8 hours.

SHRIMP & MUSHROOMS

1½ to 2 cups of shrimp
2 tablespoons of oil
2 cups of chopped celery
1 can of mushrooms, sliced
1 tablespoon of soy sauce
1 teaspoon of powdered sugar
½ teaspoon of pepper
1 tablespoon of cornstarch
½ cup of beef broth

Heat oil in a skillet. Sauté celery and onions. Add soy sauce, powdered sugar and pepper to the skillet and stir carefully. Cook for 5 minutes. Add a little water to cornstarch and make a thin paste. Add the paste, broth and shrimp to the pan. Simmer to thicken gravy and heat shrimp.

SHRIMP FOO YUNG

4 cups of cooked white rice
4 eggs beaten
1½ cups of shrimp, chopped
1 cup of onion, diced
1 cup of celery, diced
2 tablespoons of oil

Pour oil in skillet and heat. Combine all ingredients and cook.

SHRIMP FRIED RICE

2 cups of chopped shrimp
4 cups of cooked rice, cold
1 tablespoon of salt
¼ cup of oil
2 tablespoons of soy sauce
Pepper to taste
2 eggs, lightly beaten (optional)

Fry shrimp in oil for 1 minute, stirring constantly. Add salt pepper and eggs. Fry over medium heat for 5 minutes, stirring constantly. Add rice and soy sauce and cook for 5 minutes.

SHRIMP OMELET

½ cup of shrimp
½ cup of mushroom soup
4 eggs, beaten
1 tablespoon of milk
Salt and pepper
Butter

Melt butter in a frying pan. Pour in beaten eggs and cook slowly with a lid on the pan. Heat shrimp and mushroom soup together in a separate pan. Flip egg mixture and place shrimp mixture on top and fold over. Cover and cook 2 minutes.

SHRIMP SCAMPI

½ pound of cleaned shrimp, fresh or frozen
4 tablespoons of butter (4 pats)
2 cloves of garlic
1 teaspoon of parsley

Put shrimp in a baking dish and cook uncovered at 375 degrees for 4 minutes. Remove from oven and drain any liquid. Slice butter over the top of shrimp the grate garlic on top and sprinkle with parsley. Cover with plastic wrap. Cook for 3 more minutes. Remove from oven and let stand for 2 minutes. Shrimp should be moist and tender. If not, pop back in the oven for 2 more minutes.

SWEET & SOUR SHRIMP

1½ pounds of fresh shrimp, cooked
¼ cup of oil
1 cup of celery, diced
1 cup of green pepper, diced
½ cup of onion, diced
2 tablespoons of flour
1½ cups of tomato juice
¼ cup of brown sugar
¼ cup of lemon juice
½ teaspoon of salt
1 tablespoon of lemon rind, grated
1 can of pineapple slices

In a skillet, sauté celery, pepper and onion in oil. Ad flour and mix well. Add tomato juice, brown sugar, salt, lemon juice and lemon rind. Cook 5 minutes. Cook for 5 minutes. Add shrimp and pineapple slices. Heat thoroughly. Serve with rice.

SAUCES

BEURRE NOIR

8 tablespoons of clarified butter
2 tablespoons of finely chopped parsley
3 tablespoons of vinegar
White pepper, freshly ground
Salt

Put butter in a skillet and warm over low heat until it turns slightly golden brown. Add parsley and vinegar. If vinegar is not available, use 1½ tablespoons of lemon juice. Salt and pepper to taste. Keep sauce warmed by hot water under the pan.

CHIVE & LEMON BUTTER

1 stick of butter, diced and room temperature
5 tablespoons of chives, chopped
Grated zest and juice from ½ lemon

Put the ingredients in a blender or food processor. Mix until thoroughly blended. Form the mixture into a roll and wrap in aluminum foil. Put in the refrigerator until firm then slice as needed.

CILANTRO COCKTAIL SAUCE

1 cup of ketchup
2 tablespoons of lime juice, fresh squeezed
1½ tablespoons of horseradish
2 tablespoons of cilantro, minced

Mix all ingredients together in a blender or food processor.

DILL SAUCE

5 tablespoons of dill, finely chopped
2 tablespoons of olive oil
1 tablespoon of lemon juice
2 cups of mayonnaise
2 tablespoons of sour cream

Put dill, olive oil and lemon juice in a blender. Run at high speed for 60 to 90 seconds. Remove mixture and combine with mayonnaise. Finally, stir in sour cream and serve with fish as a topping or a dip.

DUNGENESS CRAB SAUCE

1 cup of mayonnaise
1 cup of chili sauce
¼ cup of celery, diced fine
4 sprigs of parsley, chopped fine
2 scallions, diced fine
1 tablespoon of lemon juice
1 tablespoon of sugar
1 teaspoon of Worcestershire sauce

Combine all ingredients thoroughly and refrigerate for at least 3 hours.

EAST COAST TARTAR SAUCE

1 quart of mayonnaise
2 large dill pickles finely chopped
2 large onions finely chopped
Garlic powder, salt and pepper to taste
4 teaspoons of fresh, snipped dill
   (exclude heavy stems)

Combine ingredients and mix well. If mixture is a little too thick, thin with dill pickle juice. Refrigerate for at least 24 hours.

FISH MARINADE

½ cup of rice vinegar
½ cup of lime juice, fresh squeezed
¼ cup of oil
1 tablespoon of honey
1 tablespoon of chili oil
1 teaspoon of sesame seed

Mix all ingredients thoroughly and store in bottle that can be sealed.

HONEY GINGER SAUCE

1/3 cup of soy sauce
1/3 cup of orange juice
1 teaspoon of ground ginger
1 teaspoon of garlic powder
¼ cup of honey

Mix all ingredients thoroughly. This can be used as a sauce or a marinade.

LEMON BUTTER

8 tablespoons of clarified butter
4 teaspoons of fresh lemon juice
2 pinches of salt

Whisk all ingredients together and serve with fish, crab or lobster.

LEMON BUTTER WITH ALMONDS

½ cup of butter
½ cup of slivered almonds (optional)
1½ teaspoons of lemon juice
1½ tablespoons of parsley flakes

Place all ingredients in a small pan. Cook on a medium low setting until butter is melted. Keep stirring until butter is slightly browned.

LOBSTER SAUCE

10 ounces of lobster soup, canned
5 ounces of cream
1 tablespoon of butter

Thoroughly mix the lobster soup with cream until smooth. Add in the butter and heat to just before boiling.

ORANGE MUSTARD SAUCE

¼ cup or orange marmalade
2 tablespoons of orange marmalade
¼ cup of orange juice
2 tablespoons of orange juice
2 tablespoons of Dijon mustard

Combine all ingredients in a bowl and stir well.

PACIFIC TARTAR SAUCE

    1 cup of mayonnaise
    2 teaspoons of lemon juice
    1 tablespoon of sweet pickles, diced
    1 tablespoon of parsley, diced fine
    1 tablespoon of onion, diced fine

Mix thoroughly and serve. You may want to chill for a few hours depending on your taste.

SAGE BUTTER

1 stick of butter
2 teaspoons of olive oil
2 teaspoons of garlic
10 leaves of sage
1/8 teaspoon of salt
1/8 teaspoon of rosemary

Put olive oil and butter in a pan. When the butter is half-melted, stir in rosemary, sage, garlic and salt. Continue heating and stirring. Once butter is fully melted and warm, let stand for 2 minutes so butter can absorb the flavors.

SALMON RUB

¼ cup of dried orange peel
¼ cup of brown sugar, packed firmly
¼ cup of peppercorns
3 tablespoons of coriander seeds
2 tablespoons of cracked star anise
1 tablespoon of cumin seeds
1 tablespoon of fennel seeds
1 tablespoon of sea salt

Combine all the ingredients in a spice grinder and process to a semi-course texture. Store in an airtight bottle or jar.

SPICY GARLIC SAUCE

2 cloves of garlic
2 tablespoons of olive oil
¼ teaspoon of red pepper flakes
1 teaspoon of steak seasoning
1 teaspoon of lemon zest
2 teaspoons of lemon juice

Mix all ingredients thoroughly and heat in a pan if you like.

SEAFOOD COCKTAIL SAUCE

½ cup of chili sauce
1/3 cup of ketchup
1/3 cup of horseradish
1½ teaspoons of Worcestershire sauce

Mix all ingredients together thoroughly and enjoy.

WHITE SAUCE

4 cups of milk
7 tablespoons of butter
6 tablespoons of flour
Salt to taste

Melt half of the butter and stir in flour slowly. Gradually add in milk and stir over medium heat until sauce thickens. Add in the rest of the butter and salt to taste. If recipe makes too much sauce, cut ingredients in half.

For more information on "Flannel John's Cookbooks" and additional titles from author Tim Murphy, visit www.flanneljohn.com.

Made in the USA
Monee, IL
08 December 2022

19712562R00081